EASY THYROID MEAL PLAN 2021

THE ULTIMATE COOKBOOK TO RESTORE YOUR THYROID BALANCE AND LOSE WEIGHT

Table of Contents

Chapter 1.   Thyroid Healing Diet

How Does It Work?

Several studies have been carried out on the effect of our eating habits on our health. Results prove that the type of food we consume into our body can either make or mar our health. Excessive consumption of fatty foods and junk can lead to heart diseases or obesity. In contrast, fruits and vegetables are known to boost the immune system.

Based on this, researchers and nutritionists worldwide are studying the components of food and what makes them good for consumption. And also how a combination of them can be used to promote health or manage diseases.

The Thyroid Healing Diet involves the consumption of foods known to improve the thyroid's health. Such foods contain trace amounts of iodine, selenium, zinc, and other elements known to promote thyroid hormone production. When consumed in the right quantities, these foods are broken down, and the necessary elements are transported via the bloodstream to the thyroid, where they assist the thyroid in performing its function.

Cautions You Need to Know When Following the Thyroid Healing Diet

t's important to note that the foods recommended nder a thyroid-healing diet cannot replace drugs when : comes to treating a Thyroid disorder. They only assist ne drug therapy and help manage the thyroid when ne drug treatment plan is completed.

)o not stop taking your drugs because of the diet. This nay put you in danger!

lso, it is noteworthy to mention that the foods have to e consumed in moderation because excess onsumption will only have the opposite effect. The resence of a high concentration of these elements in ne bloodstream will result in Hyperthyroidism.

Vhile you are trying to manage the effects of one ondition, do not create another condition!

Tips for a Successful Thyroid Healing Diet

imply following a Thyroid healing diet may not lead to uccessful management therapy. Some guidelines need o be obeyed and understood before the therapy can be effective. The most important of those guidelines include;

Avoid Heavily Processed Foods

Recently, a lot of companies manufacturing processed foods spent tremendous amounts of marketing dollars to convince people about the "health benefits" of their products. Most of these claims are false and such products should not be considered when designing a healing diet. Try your best to use fresh vegetables and unprocessed animal products for your meals.

Use Iodized Salt

Not all salts are healthy for Thyroid-disorder patients. The best salt recommended for thyroid patients and almost everyone is Iodized salt.

Note: in the places where salt is listed as part of the ingredients in this book, it's referring to Iodized salt.

Avoid Sugar and Fatty foods

In general, consuming large amounts of sugars and fat is not healthy for the body. However, the craving for sugar and junks is bound to show up, especially if you are an emotional eater. The key is to find healthier substitutes for these foods. The Appetizers, Drinks, and Desserts listed in this book are healthy alternatives for processed junks.

Reduce Caffeine Intake

Caffeine, being a powerful stimulant, is dangerous if consumed daily. While practicing healthy eating, reduce the number of caffeinated drinks you take daily.

Chapter 2.   Food Guide of Thyroid Healing Diet

All the recipes of the thyroid healing diet contain ingredients that can be grown in a garden or purchased at a local grocery store. There are three categories of food when planning a Thyroid Healing Diet, these are:

- Excellent Foods
- Moderate Foods
- Worst Foods

These three categories have only one thing in common excess consumption of any of the foods in each category is bad for your thyroid. Exercise moderation when eating.

The Best Foods for your Thyroid (Excellent and Moderate)

Excellent Foods

These are the foods that should appear more frequentl in your diets. They are proven to have good effects on the state of your thyroid. Examples of food in this category include:

- Greens: beet greens, chicory, dandelion, amaranth, etc.

- Fish and seafood: tuna, sardines, salmon, shrimps, shellfish, tilapia, clams, scallops, crabs, mussels, oysters, etc.
- Nuts and Seeds: brazil nuts, walnuts, pumpkin seeds, hazelnuts, hemp seeds, sesame seeds, cashew nuts, sunflower seeds, macadamia nuts, etc.
- Poultry: Chicken, turkey, duck, etc.
- Poultry products: chicken eggs, turkey eggs, quail eggs, duck eggs, etc.
- Dairy products: yogurt, Parmesan cheese, Greek yogurt, fresh mozzarella, etc.
- Animal foods: extra-lean ground beef, lamb, pork chops, etc.
- Healthy fats: extra-virgin olive oil, coconut oil, etc.

Moderate Foods

hese are excellent foods for your thyroid but should be onsumed sparingly as high amounts could also be armful to your thyroid.

- Vegetables: cauliflower, broccoli, kale, cabbage, Brussel sprouts, spinach, beets, okra, etc.
- Fruits: strawberries, peaches, pears, etc.
- Tubers: sweet potatoes, cassava, etc.
- Legumes: soybeans, soy milk, edamame beans, tofu, tempeh, etc.
- Herbs and spices: regular salt.

- Fish and seafood: swordfish, shark, mackerel, kingfish, etc.
- Nuts and Seeds: peanuts, pine nuts, millets, etc.

The Worst Foods to Avoid for Your Thyroid.

These are foods that should be avoided at all costs when eating to manage thyroid disorders. They include

- Added Sugar: ice cream, pure chocolate, cotton candy, candies, sugar (brown, white, etc.), pastries, sweets, etc.
- Refined Grains: white bread, regular pasta, pizza dough, etc.
- Trans fats: margarine, sausages, processed meats, etc.
- Refined Oil: canola oil, cottonseed oil, soybean oil, etc.
- Highly processed food products

To avoid purchasing these unhealthy foods mistakenly, you have to scrutinize the labels of every packaged food you buy. Some packaged food producers try to trick people by wrongfully tagging their foods 100% natural; however, they cannot lie in their products' labels. All the ingredients and chemicals used in the manufacturing will be listed in the labels; do well to go through before purchasing.

Advice for Drinks

Excessive alcohol consumption is known to harm health in general, and the thyroid is not an exception. The Thyroid Healing Diet does not restrict you from consuming alcohol. However, it advises you also to practice moderation.

A single bottle of beer won't harm you, but frequent consumption of a whole bottle of vodka will not just affect your liver but also your thyroid. Studies have shown that alcohol addicts have higher chances of developing hypothyroidism. Therefore, when it comes to alcohol, tread carefully, and practice minimalism.

Chapter 3.   Breakfast Recipes

1. Zucchini Egg Casserole

Preparation Time: 10 minutes

Cooking Time: 30 minutes

Servings: 8

Ingredients:

- 10 eggs
- 3 cherry tomatoes, halved
- 1/2 cup of mushrooms, sliced
- 1/3 cup of ham, chopped
- 1 small zucchini, sliced into rounds
- 1/2 cup of spinach
- 2/3 cup of heavy cream
- Pepper
- Salt

Directions:

1. Preheat the oven to 350 ºF. Grease 9*13-inch pan and set aside.

2. In a large bowl, whisk the eggs with heavy cream, pepper, and salt. Stir in tomatoes, mushrooms, ham, zucchini, and spinach.

3. Pour egg mixture in prepared pan and bake for 30-35 minutes.

4. Serve and enjoy.

Nutrition:

- Calories: 134 kcal

- Fat: 9.8 g

- Carbohydrates: 3.4 g

- Sugar: 2 g

- Protein: 8.8 g

- Cholesterol: 222 mg

2. Sausage Egg Omelet

Preparation Time: 10 minutes

Cooking Time: 23 minutes

Servings: 12

Ingredients:

- 7 eggs

- 1 tsp. of mustard

- 2 cups of cheddar cheese, shredded

- 3/4 cup of heavy whipping cream

- 1/4 onion, chopped

- 1/2 green bell pepper, chopped

- 1 lb. of breakfast sausage

- 1/4 tsp. of pepper

- 1/2 tsp. of salt

Directions:

1. Preheat the oven to 350 ºF. Grease 9*13-inch casserole dish and set aside.

2. Brown the sausage in a pan. Add onion and bell pepper and cook until onion is softened. Remove pan from heat.

3. In a bowl, whisk eggs with mustard, 1 3/4 cups of cheese, cream, pepper, and salt.

4. Spread the sausage mixture into the prepared casserole. Pour egg mixture on top of the sausage mixture and top with remaining cheese.

5. Bake for 20-23 minutes.

6. Serve and enjoy.

Nutrition:

- Calories: 271 kcal

- Fat: 22.4 g

- Carbohydrates: 1.4 g

- Sugar: 0.7 g

- Protein: 15.6 g

- Cholesterol: 157 mg

3. Easy Cheese Quiche

Preparation Time: 10 minutes

Cooking Time: 45 minutes

Servings: 6

Ingredients:

- 12 eggs

- 12 tbsp. of butter, melted

- 4 oz. of cream cheese, softened

- 8 oz. of cheddar cheese, grated

- Pepper

- Salt

Directions:

1. Spread cheddar cheese into the 9-5-inch pie pan.

2. Add eggs, cream cheese, butter, pepper, and salt into the blender and blend until well combined.

3. Pour egg mixture over cheese in pie pan and bake at 325 ºF for 45 minutes.

4. Slice and serve.

Nutrition:

- Calories: 548 kcal

- Fat: 50.9 g

- Carbohydrates: 1.7 g

- Sugar: 0.9 g

- Protein: 22.2 g

- Cholesterol: 449 mg

4. Broccoli Egg Bake

Preparation Time: 10 minutes

Cooking Time: 30 minutes

Servings: 6

Ingredients:

- 12 eggs

- 2 cups of broccoli florets, chopped

- 1/2 cup of cheddar cheese, shredded

- 3/4 tsp. of onion powder

- 1/2 cup of unsweetened coconut milk

- Pepper

- Salt

Directions:

1. Preheat the oven to 350 ºF. Grease 9*13-inch-baking dish.

2. In a bowl, whisk the eggs with cheese, onion powder, milk, pepper, and salt. Stir in broccoli.

3. Pour egg mixture into the prepared dish and bake for 30 minutes.

4. Slice and serve.

Nutrition:

- Calories: 221 kcal

- Fat: 16.7 g

- Carbohydrates: 4.2 g

- Sugar: 2 g

- Protein: 14.8 g

- Cholesterol: 337 mg

5. Ranch Breakfast Quiche

Preparation Time: 10 minutes

Cooking Time: 55 minutes

Servings: 6

Ingredients:

- 8 eggs

- 1 cup of sour cream

- 1 tbsp. of ranch seasoning

- 1 1/2 cups of cheddar cheese, shredded

- 1 lb. of ground Italian sausage

Directions:

1. Preheat the oven to 350 ºF.

2. Brown the sausage in an oven-safe skillet and drain well.

3. In a bowl, whisk eggs with ranch seasoning and sour cream. Stir in cheddar cheese.

4. Pour egg mixture over sausage in skillet. Cover skillet with foil.

5. Bake for 30 minutes. Remove foil and bake fo
   25 minutes more.

6. Serve and enjoy.

Nutrition:

- Calories: 511 kcal

- Fat: 40.6 g

- Carbohydrates: 3.8 g

- Sugar: 2 g

- Protein: 29 g

- Cholesterol: 318 mg

6. Chicken Cheese Quiche

Preparation Time: 10 minutes

Cooking Time: 45 minutes

Servings: 4

Ingredients:

- 8 eggs

- 1/2 tsp. of oregano

- 1/4 tsp. of onion powder

- 1/4 tsp. of garlic powder

- 1/4 cup of mozzarella cheese, shredded

- 5 oz. of cooked chicken breast, chopped

- 1/4 tsp. of pepper

- 1/2 tsp. of salt

Directions:

1. Preheat the oven to 350 °F.

2. In a bowl, whisk the eggs with oregano, onion powder, pepper, and salt. Stir in cheese and chicken.

3. Pour the egg mixture into a pie pan and bake for 35-45 minutes.

4. Slice and serve.

Nutrition:

- Calories: 173 kcal

- Fat: 10 g

- Carbohydrates: 1.2 g

- Sugar: 0.8 g

- Protein: 19.2 g

- Cholesterol: 351 mg

7. Turkey Cheese Frittata

Preparation Time: 10 minutes

Cooking Time: 25 minutes

Servings: 8

Ingredients:

- 8 eggs

- 8 oz. of turkey deli meat

- 2 tbsp. of cheddar cheese, shredded

- 2 tbsp. of parmesan cheese, shredded

- 1/2 tsp. of oregano

- 1/2 tsp. of thyme

- 1/4 tsp. of pepper

- 1/4 tsp. of salt

Directions:

1. Preheat the oven to 350 ºF.

2. Line an 8-inch skillet with the turkey deli meat.

3. In a bowl, whisk the eggs with oregano, thyme, pepper, and salt. Pour egg mixture over meat.

4. Sprinkle the parmesan cheese and cheddar cheese on top.

5. Bake for 20-25 minutes.

6. Serve and enjoy.

Nutrition:

- Calories: 108 kcal

- Fat: 6 g

- Carbohydrates: 1.2 g

- Sugar: 0.4 g

- Protein: 11.8 g

- Cholesterol: 178 mg

Chapter 4.   Lunch Recipes

8. Fiery Fish Tacos with Crunchy Corn Salsa

Preparation Time: 30 minutes

Cooking Time: 10 minutes

Servings: 6

Ingredients:

- 1 small red onion, diced

- 1 cup of jicama, peeled and diced

- 1/2 cup of red bell pepper, diced

- 1 cup of cilantro leaves, chopped

- 1 small lime, zested and juiced

- 2 Tbsps. of cayenne pepper,

- 1 Tbsps. of ground black pepper

- 2 Tbsps. of salt,

- 6 fillets of tilapia, 4 oz. each

- 2 Tbsps. of extra virgin olive oil

- 12 corn tortillas, lightly heated

- 2 Tbsps. of sour cream

Directions:

1. Preheat the grill and lightly oil the grates.

2. Mix the corn tortillas, onion, bell pepper, cilantro, lime juice, zest, and jicama together in a medium bowl. This will serve as the corn salsa.

3. In another bowl, mix the cayenne pepper, salt, black pepper, and olive oil. This will serve as the glaze.

4. Brush the glaze on each fillet. Make sure both sides are coated.

5. Arrange the fillets on the grate and grill for 3 minutes on each side.

6. For a serving, arrange a fillet, corn salsa, and sour cream on two corn tortillas.

Nutrition:

- Calories: 351 kcal

- Carbs: 40g

- Fat:10g

- Protein: 29g

9. Salmon Chowder

Preparation Time: 30 minutes

Cooking Time: 10 minutes

Servings: 8

Ingredients:

- 3 Tbsps. of cream cheese
- 2 cups of chicken broth
- 1 tsp. of ground garlic
- 2 medium potatoes, diced
- 15 oz. of can creamed corn
- 2 carrots, sliced
- 1 tsp. of salt
- 1 tsp. of ground black pepper
- 1/2 cup of celery, chopped
- 1 tsp. of dried dill weed
- 2 medium onions, chopped
- 2 canned salmon, 16 ounces each
- 12 oz. of evaporated milk

- 1/2-pound Cheddar cheese, shredded

Directions:

1. Use cream cheese to sauté onions, garlic, and celery until onions turn translucent.

2. Stir in broth, potatoes, potatoes, carrots, pepper, salt, and dill. Bring to a boil, then lower heat and simmer for 20 minutes.

3. Add salmon, milk, corn, and cheese. Wait until cheese melts completely, then remove from heat. Serve.

Nutrition:

- Calories: 490 kcal

- Carbs: 27g

- Fat: 26

- Protein: 29g

10.   Baked Coconut Shrimp

Preparation Time: 15 minutes

Cooking Time: 15 minutes

Servings: 4

Ingredients:

- 1-pound of large shrimp, deveined and peeled
- 1 tsp. of salt
- 3/4 tsp. of cayenne pepper
- 2 cups of sweetened coconut flakes
- 3 egg whites, beaten until foamy
- 1/3 cup of cornstarch

Directions:

1. Preheat oven to 400 °F. Coat baking sheet with non-stick spray.

2. In a small bowl, mix cornstarch, cayenne pepper, and salt. Set aside.

3. Pour the coconut flakes into a separate bowl and set them aside.

4. Wash the shrimps, then dry with paper towels. Coat each shrimp one at a time by

dredging in cornstarch mixture, then dipping it into the egg foam before finally rolling it on the coconut flakes. Make sure each shrimp is well coated before arranging them on the prepared baking sheet.

5. Bake until shrimps turn pink and coconut is browned. This will take about 15-20 minutes. Remember to flip shrimps after 10 minutes.

6. Allow to cool, then serve.

Nutrition:

- Calories: 310 kcal

- Carbs: 27g

- Fat: 11

- Protein: 22g

11.   Broiled Scallops

Preparation Time: 5 minutes

Cooking Time: 8 minutes

Servings: 3

Ingredients:

- 1-1/2 pounds of bay scallops
- 1 tsp. of garlic salt
- 2 Tbsps. of cream cheese, melted
- 2 Tbsps. of lemon juice

Directions:

1. Switch on the broiler.

2. Rinse scallops and arrange them in a baking pan. Sprinkle with garlic salt, lemon juice, and cream cheese.

3. Broil for 6-8 minutes and remove from oven when scallops turn golden.

4. Serve with melted cream cheese on the side for dipping.

Nutrition:

- Calories: 273 kcal

- Carbs: 7g

- Fat: 9

- Protein: 38g

12.   Rice and Tuna Salad

Preparation Time: 1 hour 10 minutes

Cooking Time: 0 minutes

Servings: 6

Ingredients:

- 2 cup of white rice, cooked

- 1 can (5 oz.) of tuna, drained

- 1 can (8 oz.) of sweet corn, drained

- 2 Tbsps. of sweet pickle relish

- 1/2 cup of creamy salad dressing

Directions:

1. Pour the cooked rice into a large bowl.

2. Add the tuna, sweet corn, pickle, and salad dressing. Toss, then refrigerate for 1 hour.

3. Serve.

Nutrition:

- Calories: 234 kcal

- Carbs: 36g

- Fat: 6

- Protein: 9g

Chapter 5.   Vegan & Vegetarian Recipes

13.   Cuban Black Beans

Preparation Time: 5 minutes

Cooking Time: 35 minutes

Servings: 4

Ingredients:

- 1 medium green bell pepper
- 4-1/4 cooked no-salt-added black beans
- 2 cups of no-salt-added tomato juice
- 1 cup of no-salt-added tomato sauce
- 4 cloves of garlic, minced
- 1 tsp. of cumin
- 1/2 tsp. of ginger powder
- 1/3 tsp. of ground black pepper
- 1/3 cup of cilantro
- 1 Tbsps. of red wine vinegar
- 1-1/2 cup of dried beans

- 1 Tbsps. of water

Directions:

1. Add 1 tablespoon of water to a large saucepan, then place on medium heat.

2. Add the onions and bell pepper to the water and cook until tender. This will take about 2 minutes.

3. Add the rest of the ingredients except cilantro and vinegar. Allow to boil, then cover and reduce the heat. Allow to simmer for 25 minutes, then stir in the cilantro and vinegar.

4. Serve.

Nutrition:

- Calories: 255kcal

- Carbs: 46g

- Fat: 3g

- Protein: 15g

14.   Avocado and Mango Lettuce Wrap

Preparation Time: 10 minutes

Cooking Time: 0 minutes

Servings: 2

Ingredients:

- 1 medium mango, diced
- 1 medium tomato, chopped
- 1 large ripe avocado, peeled and pitted
- 1 medium cucumber, diced and peeled
- 1 Tbsps. of lime juice
- 6 leaves of romaine lettuce (or collard green)

Directions:

1. Mash the avocado to form a cream in a bowl. Add in the diced mango, tomato, cucumber, and lime juice, then mix.

2. Spread the avocado cream cheese mixture on each of the lettuce leaves and roll to form a wrap.

3. Serve

Nutrition:

- Calories: 281kcal

- Carbs: 36g

- Fat: 16g

- Protein: 8g

Chapter 6.   Dinner Recipes

15.   White Bean Chicken Chili

Preparation Time: 10 minutes

Cooking Time: 25 minutes

Servings: 9

Ingredients:

- 2 Tbsps. of extra virgin olive oil
- 1 large onion, chopped
- 2 cloves of garlic, minced
- 15 oz. of chicken broth
- 18. 75 oz. of tomatillos, chopped and drained
- 16 oz. of tomatoes, diced
- 7 oz. of green chiles, diced
- 1/2 tsp. of dried oregano
- 1/2 tsp. of ground coriander seed
- 1 tsp. of salt
- 15 oz. of white beans
- 1/4 ground cumin

- 1-pound of cooked chicken, diced

- 2 ears of fresh corn

- 1/3 parmesan cheese, grated

Directions:

1. Pour the olive oil into a large-sized non-stick pot and place over medium heat. Once the oil starts to sizzle, add the onions and garlic, then stir until onions turn translucent.

2. Stir in the tomatoes, broth, chiles, tomatillos, and spices. Allow to boil, then reduce heat, and simmer for 10 minutes.

3. Stir in the corn, beans, and chicken, then simmer for 5 minutes.

4. Season with pepper and salt. Stir.

5. Top with parmesan cheese and serve.

Nutrition:

- Calories: 220 kcal

- Carbs: 6.1g

- Fat: 21.2g

- Protein: 20.1g

16.   Black-eyed Pea Gumbo

Preparation Time: 15 minutes

Cooking Time: 55 minutes

Servings: 4

Ingredients:

- 1 Tbsps. of extra virgin olive oil
- 1 large onion, chopped
- 2 cloves of garlic, minced
- 2 cups of chicken broth
- 14 oz. of tomatoes, diced
- 10 oz. of tomatoes and green chiles, diced
- 60 oz. of black-eyed peas
- 1 medium green bell pepper, chopped
- 1 cup of brown rice
- 5 stalks of celery, chopped

Directions:

1. Pour the olive oil into a large-sized non-stick pot and place over medium heat. Once the oil starts to sizzle, add the onions, garlic, celery,

and pepper, then stir until celery becomes
tender.

2. Stir in the rice, chicken broth, black-eyed pea
   with juice, diced tomatoes, and diced
   tomatoes and chiles. Allow to boil, then
   reduce heat, and simmer for 45 minutes.

3. Serve.

Nutrition:

- Calories: 187 kcal

- Carbs: 23.1g

- Fat: 3.8g

- Protein: 15.3g

17. Rutabaga Stew

Preparation Time: 20 minutes

Cooking Time: 4hours 5 minutes

Servings: 4

Ingredients:

- 1 Tbsps. of extra-virgin olive oil
- 1-1/2 pounds of chicken, shredded
- 4 rutabagas, diced and peeled
- 4 medium-sized beets, peeled and diced
- 3 stalks of celery, diced
- 4 medium carrots, diced
- 1 small red onion, diced
- Water, to cover

Directions:

1. Pour the oil into a large soup pot, then place over medium heat.

2. When the oil starts to sizzle, add the chicken. Leave to fry for 3-5 minutes, or until both sides turn brown.

3. Add rutabagas, carrots, beets, red onion, and celery to the pot, then pour enough water to completely cover the vegetable mixture.

4. Reduce the heat and allow to simmer for 4 hours. Keep the vegetables submerged by adding water periodically.

5. Serve.

Nutrition:

- Calories: 111 kcal

- Carbs: 12.9g

- Fat: 2.1g

- Protein: 10.7g

18.   Tomato-Curry Lentil Stew

Preparation Time: 10 minutes

Cooking Time: 50 minutes

Servings: 2

Ingredients:

- 1 cup of water

- 1/2 cup of dry lentils

- 5 oz. of stewed tomatoes

- 1 small onion, chopped

- 2 stalks of celery, chopped

- 1/3 tsp. of curry powder

- 1/2 tsp. of salt

- 3 cloves of garlic, minced

- 1/2 tsp. of ground black pepper

Directions:

1. Mix lentils and water in a medium-sized pot and place on medium heat to boil.

2. Reduce the heat, stir in the celery, onion, and tomatoes and simmer for 45 minutes. Stir the

stew every 15 minutes and add water if necessary. In the last 15 minutes, add the spices: salt, pepper, garlic, and curry.

3. After the 45 minutes is complete, remove from heat and serve.

Nutrition:

- Calories: 206 kcal

- Carbs: 36.9g

- Fat: 0.8g

- Protein: 13.7g

Chapter 7.   Appetizers

19.   Vegetable Tagine

Preparation Time: 10 minutes

Cooking Time: 1 hour

Servings: 4

Ingredients:

- 1 large onion, thinly sliced
- 2 medium carrots, diced
- 1 medium red bell pepper, chopped
- 1 tsp. of cinnamon
- 1 tsp. of turmeric
- 2 medium tomatoes, diced
- 1/2 dried apricot
- 1 large tomato, sliced
- 1 clove of garlic, minced
- 1/2 cup of no-salt-added vegetable broth
- 1 cup of water
- 1 medium zucchini, diced

- 1 Tbsps. of lemon juice

- 1/2 cup of dried beans

- 2 Tbsps. of cilantro, minced

- 1-1/2 garbanzo beans, cooked

Directions:

1. Soak the apricots in hot water for 20 minutes. Add enough water to cover.

2. Pour the 1 cup of water into a large saucepan and place over medium heat. Add the bell pepper, carrots, and onion. Cover and bring t a boil.

3. Once boiled, stir in the zucchini, cinnamon, tomatoes, turmeric, garlic, and vegetable broth. Lower the heat and simmer for 25 minutes.

4. Drain the apricots, chop, then add to the pan Also, add the soaking water, lemon juice, raisins, and garbanzo beans. Cook for 5 minutes.

5. Add the cilantro. Stir.

6. Serve.

Nutrition:

- Calories: 242kcal

- Carbs: 48g

- Fat: 2.9g

- Protein: 12g

20.   Orange Zest Chard

Preparation Time: 5 minutes

Cooking Time: 10 minutes

Servings: 4

Ingredients:

- 2 shallots, chopped

- 2 cloves of garlic, minced

- 1 medium orange, juiced, and zested

- 2 bunches of Swiss chard, leaves and stem, separated and chopped

- 1/4 tsp. of allspice

- 1/4 tsp. of chipotle chili flakes

- 2 Tbsps. of blood orange vinegar

Directions:

1. Stir-fry the garlic, shallots, and chard stems in a non-stick pan for about 5 minutes. Stir continuously to avoid burning.

2. Add the orange juice and zest, chili flakes, and allspice.

3. Deglaze the pan with vinegar, then add the chard leaves. Steam for about 3 minutes.

4. Serve.

Nutrition:

- Calories: 35kcal

- Carbs: 7g

- Fat: 0.2g

- Protein: 2g

21.   Seaweed Salad

Preparation Time: 10 minutes

Cooking Time: - minutes

Servings: 4

Ingredients:

- 3/4 oz. of dried wakame seaweed, cut
- 3 Tbsps. of rice vinegar, unseasoned
- 3 Tbsps. of Worcestershire sauce
- 1 Tbsps. of sesame oil
- Red pepper flakes
- 1 tsp ginger, grated
- 1/2 tsp. of garlic, minced
- 2 scallions, thinly sliced
- 1/4 cup of carrots, shredded
- 2 Tbsps. of cilantro, chopped
- 1 Tbsps. of sesame seeds, toasted

Directions:

1. Prepare warm water in a medium bowl and soak the seaweed in it for 5 minutes. Make sure the bowl is covered.

2. Remove the seaweed from the soaking water and rinse. Be sure to squeeze out any excess water.

3. In a separate bowl, mix the vinegar, sesame oil, soy sauce, pepper flakes, garlic, and ginger. Then add the squeezed seaweed, carrots, scallions, and cilantro. Toss until well combined.

4. Sprinkle the sesame seeds on the salad.

5. Serve.

Nutrition:

- Calories: 291kcal

- Carbs: 38g

- Fat: 1.5g

- Protein: 19g

22.   Swiss Chard and Italian Beans

Preparation Time: 10 minutes

Cooking Time: - minutes

Servings: 4

Ingredients:

- 6 cloves of garlic, minced

- 1/2 cup of dried beans

- 1/2 tsp. of no-salt Italian seasoning powder

- 1-1/2 cups of red kidney beans

- 3 large tomatoes, chopped

- 1-pound of Swiss chard

- 1-1/2 tomato sauce, no-salt

Directions:

1. Mix all the ingredients in a pot and place over low heat. Simmer until chard becomes soft. Stir continuously.

Nutrition:

- Calories: 174kcal

- Carbs: 34g

- Fat: 1g

- Protein: 13g

23.   Spinach with Mushrooms and Leeks

Preparation Time: 5 minutes

Cooking Time: 15 minutes

Servings: 4

Ingredients:

- 8 oz. of mushroom, sliced

- 2 cloves of garlic, minced

- 10 oz. of spinach

- 2 medium leeks, chopped

- 1/3 tsp. of dried thyme

- 1/4 tsp. of black pepper

- 1 Tbsps. of cooking sherry

- 1 Tbsps. of nutritional yeast

- 1/3 tsp. of ground red pepper

Directions:

1. Add 2 tablespoons of water to a large skillet, and place over medium heat. Add the mushrooms, garlic, and leeks. Boil until water evaporates completely. This will take about 4 minutes.

2. Add the spinach, then wait until the spinach is wilted enough before you add the thyme, red pepper, and black pepper. Cover, then wait for 2 minutes to add the vinegar and nutritional yeast. Stir.

3. Serve.

Nutrition:

- Calories: 139 kcal

- Carbs: 26g

- Fat: 1.2g

- Protein: 11g

Chapter 8.   Meat Recipes

24.   Country Beef Stew

Preparation Time: 5 minutes

Cooking Time: 2 hours

Servings: 8

Ingredients:

- 2-pound boneless beef chuck, cut into 1-inch cubes
- 2 medium carrot, sliced
- 2 Tbsps. of extra-virgin olive oil
- 1 medium onion, chopped
- 1-1/2 cups of water
- 1 Tbsps. of Worcestershire sauce
- 3/4 tsp. of tarragon
- 1/2 tsp. of black pepper
- 2 cups of canned no-salt-added tomatoes
- 1 clove garlic, minced

Directions:

1. In a medium skillet, brown half of the beef. This will take about five minutes.

2. Remove the beef carefully, then brown the other half of the beef. Once done, join both browned beef together in the skillet.

3. Stir in the water, Worcestershire sauce, tomatoes, onions, tarragon, garlic, and black pepper. Bring to a boil.

4. Lower the heat and allow to simmer, covered, for about an hour. Add carrots, simmer for 20 minutes, then increase the heat and add beans. Cook for 5 minutes.

5. Serve.

utrition:

- Calories: 587 kcal

- Carbs: 42g

- Fat: 26g

- Protein: 46g

25. Irish Stew

Preparation Time: 5 minutes

Cooking Time: 1 hour 30 minutes

Servings: 8

Ingredients:

- 2 pounds beef stew meat
- 1/4 cup of cornstarch
- 4 potatoes, cut into quarters
- 1 cup of a medium onion, sliced
- 12 oz. of dark beer
- 1/2 cup of water
- 2 cups of beef broth
- 3 Tbsps. of no-salt-added tomato paste
- 1 clove garlic, minced
- 2 medium carrot, sliced
- 2 turnips, cut into quarters
- 1 tsp. of rosemary
- 1/4 tsp. of black pepper, grounded

- 2 bay leaves

Directions:

1. Pour all the ingredients (except cornstarch and water) into a pot and cook until meat and potatoes are tender. This may take up to an hour.

2. Mix the cornstarch and water in a bowl, then add to the pot of stew. Cook for about 30 minutes until the soup is well thickened.

3. Serve.

Nutrition:

- Calories: 420 kcal

- Carbs: 43g

- Fat: 12g

- Protein: 43g

26.   Eggplant Stew

Preparation Time: 5 minutes

Cooking Time: 1 hour

Servings: 6

Ingredients:

- 1-1/2 pounds of beef stew meat, cubed

- 2 Tbsps. of extra-virgin olive oil

- 2 cups of no-salt-added canned tomatoes

- 1 medium onion, chopped

- 1/2 tsp. of oregano

- 1/2 tsp. of basil

- 1/2 tsp. of cumin

- 1/4 tsp. of red pepper flakes

- 1/2 tsp. of garlic powder

- 1 cup of water

- 2 Tbsps. of no-salt-added tomato paste

- 1 cup of white wine

- 1 potato, peeled and cubed

- 1 eggplant, peeled and cubed

- 2 mushrooms, sliced

Directions:

1. In a medium skillet, brown half of the beef. This will take about five minutes.

2. Remove the beef carefully, then brown the other half of the beef. Once done, drain the oil and join both browned beef together in the skillet.

3. Stir in water, tomato paste, tomatoes, onions, and spices. Bring to a boil.

4. Lower the heat, keep covered, and simmer for 45 minutes.

5. Add potatoes and wine, stir and keep simmering for 10 more minutes.

6. Add in the cubed eggplants and mushrooms. Simmer for 20 minutes and remove from heat.

7. Serve.

Nutrition:

- Calories: 504 kcal

- Carbs: 23g

- Fat: 27g

- Protein: 36g

27.   Peasant Soup

Preparation Time: - minutes

Cooking Time: 45 minutes

Servings: 6

Ingredients:

- 1-pound of roast beef, chopped

- 2 cups of beef broth

- 1/2 cup of turnips, cubed

- 1-pound of canned mixed vegetables

- 1 cup of canned no-salt-added tomatoes

Directions:

1. Mix all the ingredients in a large pot and place over low heat. Simmer for 45 minutes until vegetables are tender.

2. Serve.

Nutrition:

- Calories: 198 kcal

- Carbs: 13g

- Fat: 5g

- Protein: 25g

28.   Beef and Mushroom Stew

Preparation Time: 5 minutes

Cooking Time: 1 hour

Servings: 6

Ingredients:

- 2 cups of canned no-salt-added tomatoes

- 14 oz. of beef broth

- 1/2 cup of red wine

- 1/4 tsp. of ground black pepper

- 5 medium potatoes, quartered

- 3 medium carrots, sliced

- 2 mushrooms, sliced

- 1 bay leaf

- 1/4 tsp. of dried rosemary

- 3 Tbsps. of flour

- 1/4 cup of water

- 1-1/2 pounds of beef round steak, cut into cubes

Directions:

1. Mix all the ingredients (except flour, tomatoes, and water) in a large pot and place over medium heat. Cover and cook for 1 hour

2. Mix the flour, water, and tomatoes in a small bowl.

3. Add tomatoes mixture to the pot. Cook until stew starts to thicken. This may take about 10-20 minutes

4. Serve.

Nutrition:

- Calories: 507 kcal

- Carbs: 59g

- Fat: 7g,

- Protein: 50g

Chapter 9. Chicken & Poultry Recipes

29. Chili Pronto

Preparation Time: 5 minutes

Cooking Time: 30 minutes

Servings: 4

Ingredients:

- 14-1/2 tomatoes with green chiles, diced
- 2 green bell peppers, diced
- 9 0z can of mixed vegetables
- 4-1/2 can be chopped mild green chiles
- 1 Tbsps. of chili seasoning mix
- 1-1/2 cups of cooked chicken, chopped
- 1/4 cup of fat-free sour cream
- 2 scallions, thinly sliced and white and green part only
- 2 cups of baked tortilla chips

Directions:

1. Mix the bell peppers, tomatoes, mixed vegetables, chili seasoning, and chiles in a medium saucepan. Cover and bring to a boil.

2. Lower the heat, uncover, and allow to simmer until the vegetables soften and the flavors are blended. This may take about 10 minutes.

3. Add the chicken and cook for 3 minutes. Stir periodically.

4. Split the chili into 4 small bowls. Drizzle the sour cream on the top and garnish with scallions.

5. Serve with tortilla chips.

Nutrition:

- Calories: 235kcal

- Carbs: 30g

- Fat: 4g

- Protein: 20g

30.   Easy Chili with Cheese

Preparation Time: 5 minutes

Cooking Time: 30 minutes

Servings: 4

Ingredients:

- 1 tsp. of extra virgin olive oil

- 2 tsp. of chili seasoning mix

- 14 oz. of canned tomatoes, diced

- 1 large onion, chopped

- 2 cups of corn kernels

- 1 cup of cooked chicken, chopped

- 4 flour tortillas, 6 inches each

- 1/2 cup of reduced-fat Monterey Jack cheese, shredded

Directions:

1. Add the oil to a large saucepan, then place over medium heat.

2. Add the onions to the oil and fry until translucent. This will take about 2 minutes.

3. Add the seasoning mix and cook until the aroma fills the air. Add tomatoes and boil.

4. Once boiled, lower the heat, uncover, and simmer for about three minutes. Stir in the chicken and corn. Continue to simmer for 3 minutes. Set aside.

5. Spray the non-stick spray on a large skillet and place over medium heat. Add in the tortillas separately, and cook each side for 1 minute. Cut each tortilla into shapes (usually triangles).

6. Add cheese to the chili sauce and stir until it melts completely.

7. Serve the chili with toasted tortilla triangles.

Nutrition:

- Calories: 290kcal

- Carbs: 36g

- Fat: 9g

- Protein: 19g

31.   Tarragon Chicken Salad with Orange Mayonnaise

Preparation Time: 10 minutes

Cooking Time: 0 minutes

Servings: 4

Ingredients:

- 2 tsp. of tarragon, chopped
- 1-1/2 tsp. of Dijon mustard
- 1-1/2 tsp. of apple cider vinegar
- 1 cup of seedless green grapes, halved
- 1/4 tsp. of salt
- 1/8 tsp. of black pepper
- 2 cups of shredded cooked chicken breast
- 8 Boston lettuce leaves
- 1 celery stalk, thinly sliced
- 1/4 cup of fat-free mayonnaise
- 1/4 cup of red onion, thinly sliced
- 1 navel orange
- 2 Tbsps. of walnuts, chopped

Directions:

1. Prepare the dressing by mixing the mayonnaise, mustard, salt, vinegar, tarragon and pepper in a medium bowl. Grate about 1/2 teaspoon orange zest and add to the dressing.

2. Peel and deseed the orange, then cut into 4 quarters.

3. Add the orange quarters, grapes, chicken, celery, walnuts, and onion into the dressing. Toss until well combined.

4. Share the lettuce into four equal parts. Spoor the mixed salad onto the lettuce. Serve.

Nutrition:

- Calories: 183kcal

- Carbs: 15g

- Fat: 6g

- Protein: 19g

32. Chicken-Prosciutto Bundles

Preparation Time: 5 minutes

Cooking Time: 50 minutes

Servings: 4

Ingredients:

- 4 chicken breasts

- 1 tsp. of extra virgin olive oil

- 1/4 tsp. black pepper

- 4 slices of part-skim mozzarella cheese

- 12 basil leaves

- 8 thin slices of prosciutto

Directions:

1. Preheat the oven and set it to 400 °F.

2. Make pockets on the side of each chicken by gently slicing the meat. Do not cut to reach the other side. Insert a slice of cheese and 3 basil leaves into each pocket. Sprinkle pepper on each chicken and wrap in 2 slices of prosciutto.

3. Add the olive oil to a large skillet, then place on medium-high heat. Add the chicken and fr until lightly browned. This will take about 5-6 minutes.

4. Remove the chicken from the skillet and place in the oven to bake for 15 minutes.

5. Remove from oven. Cool.

6. Serve.

Nutrition:

- Calories: 267kcal

- Carbs: 1g

- Fat: 10g

- Protein: 40g

33. Chicken, Cilantro, and Cucumber Wraps

Preparation Time: 5 minutes

Cooking Time: 30 minutes

Servings: 4

Ingredients:

- 2 cups of shredded cooked chicken breast
- 1/4 cup of low-fat mayonnaise
- 1 tsp. of ginger, minced
- 1/4 cup of cilantro, chopped
- 4 flour tortillas, 8 inches
- 1 tsp. of dark sesame oil
- 1/4 tsp. of salt
- 1 medium cucumber, diced
- 1/4 tsp. black pepper

Directions:

1. Mix the cucumber, mayonnaise, chicken, cilantro, ginger, salt, oil, and pepper in a medium bowl. Toss until well combined. Set aside for 10 minutes to allow flavors to blend.

72

2. Place a large non-stick skillet over medium heat and toast the tortillas. Make sure both sides are accounted for. Remove from heat after 2 minutes.

3. Share the chicken filling equally among the tortillas and roll them up. Divide the rolls into equal halves.

4. Serve.

Nutrition:

- Calories: 239kcal

- Carbs: 21g

- Fat: 6g

- Protein: 24g

Chapter 10.   Salads and Smoothies

34.   Blueberry Smoothie

reparation Time: 3 minutes

ooking Time: 0 minutes

ervings: 2

ngredients:

- 1 cup of blueberries

- 1/2 cup of Greek yogurt

- 1/4 tsp. of vanilla extract

- 1/2 cup of freshly squeezed orange

- 1/2 tsp. of cinnamon

- 3 ice cubes

irections:

1. Pour all the ingredients (except ice) into a blender and blend for 60 seconds.

2. Add the ice and blend until smooth. This may take another 60 seconds.

Nutrition:

- Calories: 195kcal

- Carbs: 13.9g

- Fat: 10.6g

- Protein: 7.5g

35. Guacamole Salad

Preparation Time: 5 minutes

Cooking Time: 0 minutes

Servings: 4

Ingredients:

- 2 avocados, diced

- 2 garden cucumbers, chopped

- 2 cups of tomatoes, sliced

- 1 small red/brown onion

- 2 scallions, sliced

- 1 red pepper, chopped and deseeded

- 1/2 cup of pickled jalapenos

- 1 bunch chopped coriander

- 2 Tbsps. of lime juice

- 4 Tbsps. of extra virgin olive oil

- 1 Tbsps. of apple cider vinegar

- Salt, to taste

Directions:

1. Wash the vegetable ingredients and mix the cucumber, avocados, tomatoes, onion, scallion, jalapenos, coriander, and red pepper in a medium-sized bowl.

2. Prepare the dressing in a separate bowl by mixing the lime juice, apple cider vinegar, and olive oil. Add salt and pepper as desired.

3. Serve the salad into plates and drizzle the dressing over it.

Nutrition:

- Calories: 104kcal

- Carbs: 13g

- Fat: 5.5g

- Protein: 1.2g

36.   Red Quinoa Salad

Preparation Time: 5 minutes

Cooking Time: 15 minutes

Servings: 2

Ingredients:

- 1/2 cup of red quinoa, dry

- 1 cup of water

- 1/4 cup of red onion, diced

- 1/2 cup of black beans, rinsed and drained

- 1/2 Tbsps. of extra-virgin olive oil

- 1 Tbsps. of balsamic vinegar

Directions:

1. Pour the quinoa into a bowl and rinse under cold water.

2. Transfer the quinoa into a medium-sized saucepot, add water, and place over medium heat to boil for 15 minutes.

3. Once the quinoa is ready, add the ingredients red onion, black beans, extra virgin olive oil,

and balsamic vinegar. Stir until well combined.

4. Serve.

Nutrition:

- Calories: 280kcal

- Carbs: 32g

- Fat: 10g

- Protein: 16g

Chapter 11.   Drinks

37.   Summer Squash Smoothie Infused with CBD

Preparation Time: 5 minutes

Cooking Time: 5 minutes

Servings: 2

Ingredients:

- 6 oz. of yellow squash, diced and seeded
- 4 oz. of frozen preaches
- 1/2 large banana
- 2 scoops of unflavored collagen protein powder
- 1 cup of ice
- 1 Tbsps. of lemon juice
- 1 Tbsps. of honey
- 1 tsp. of ground turmeric
- 1/16 tsp. of ground cinnamon
- 1ml CBD oil

- 1/16 tsp. of ground black pepper

- 1 large mint leaf, optional

irections:

1. Blend all the ingredients in a high-speed blender for about 60-90 seconds.

2. Serve into cups and enjoy.

utrition:

- Calories: 250 kcal

- Carbs: 41g

- Fat: 7g

- Protein: 9g

38. Watermelon Shooter Shots Infused with CBD

reparation Time: 5 minutes

ooking Time: 5 minutes

ervings: 4

Ingredients:

- 5 oz. of watermelon puree

- 2-1/2 oz. of apple cider vinegar

- 1 Tbsps. of honey

- 1 ml of CBD oil

- 1/16 tsp. of pumpkin pie spice

Directions:

1. Puree the watermelon first, if not done already, and measure out 5 oz.

2. Add the honey, apple cider vinegar, and pumpkin pie spice to the puree and blend unt smooth (usually 60-90 seconds).

3. Add the CBD and stir gently.

4. The drink is ready to be served.

Nutrition:

- Calories: 30 kcal

- Carbs: 7g

- Fat: 0g

- Protein: 0g

Chapter 12.   Top Superfood Recipes for the Brain

39.   Apple Snickers Salad

Preparation Time: 5 Minutes

Cooking Time: 5 Minutes

Servings: 4

Ingredients:

- 4 large green apples

- ½ cup of milk

- ½ cup caramel

- 2 snickers bars

- 8 oz. of whip cream

- 1 instant vanilla pudding

Directions:

1. Cut up apples and snickers and mix in.

2. Mix milk and vanilla pudding, pour it into the apples, and garnish caramel.

3. Serve cold.

Nutrition:

- Calories: 216 kcal

- Fat: 89g

- Carbohydrates: 323g

- Sodium: 775 mg

- Cholesterol: 46 mg

- Protein: 30g

40.   Oat Meal Porridge

Preparation Time: 15 Minutes

Cooking Time: 15 Minutes

Servings: 4

Ingredients:

- 1-liter of water

- 1 cup of Oatmeal

- Sugar, Milk, or cream, Black grapes for garnishing

- Salt to taste

Directions:

1. In a saucepan, take water to boil.

2. Pour the oatmeal into the boiling water; stir it continuously to prevent any lumps.

3. Add the salt and reduce the heat to low for 30 minutes; stir occasionally.

4. Serve with grapes, sugar, and milk or cream.

Nutrition:

- Calories: 117 kcal

- Carbohydrates: 66.3 g

- Sugar: 36 g

- Fat: 6.9g

- Fiber: 10.6 g

- Protein: 16.9 g

41.   Red Beans and Rice

Preparation Time: 30 Minutes

Cooking Time: 30 Minutes

Servings: 4

Ingredients:

- 1 can of kidney beans

- 4 ½ cups of water

- 1 tablespoon of olive oil

- 1 ½ cups of tomato sauce

- ½ teaspoon of dried oregano and dried basil

- Salt and pepper to taste

- 2 cups of white rice (uncooked)

- 5 teaspoons of adobo seasoning

Directions:

1. In a pan, pour ½ cup of water, oil, kidney beans, tomato sauce, oregano, basil, and adobo.

2. Simmer on low heat for 25 mins or until the beans get boiled.

3. Serve hot beans over the rice.

4. On the other side, take 4 cups of water and boil it.

5. Then pour rice and stir. Simmer on low heat for 10 mins or until the rice gets cooked. Add 3 teaspoons of adobo.

Nutrition:

- Calories: 511

- Fat: 5.1g

- Sodium: 710 mg

- Carbohydrates: 101g

- Sugar: 46 g

- Fiber: 32 g

- Protein: 14.5g

- Calcium: 8.2%

42.   Fresh Broccoli Salad

Preparation Time: 15 Minutes

Cooking Time: 15 Minutes

Servings: 4

Ingredients:

- 2 heads of fresh broccoli

- 1 red onion

- 1/2-pound of bacon

- 3/4 cup of raisins

- 3/4 cup of sliced almonds

- 1 cup of mayonnaise

- 1/2 cup of white sugar

- 2 tablespoons of white wine vinegar

Directions:

1. Put the bacon in a deep skillet and let it cook over medium-high heat, and crumble it after it cools.

2. Cut the broccoli into small pieces and chop the onion into thin bite-size slices.

3. Combine with the bacon, raisins, your favorite nuts and blend well.

4. To make the dressing, add the mayonnaise with the sugar and pour the vinegar together until smooth.

5. Stir the dressing into the salad, let chill, and serve.

Nutrition:

- Calories: 374 kcal

- Fat: 27.2 g

- Carbohydrates: 28.5 g

- Sugar: 7 g

- Fiber: 18 g

- Protein: 7.3 g

- Cholesterol: 18 mg

- Sodium: 353 mg

43. Dark Chocolate Truffles

Preparation Time: 10 Minutes

Cooking Time: 10 Minutes

Servings: 4

Ingredients:

- 1 cup of heavy cream

- 2 tablespoons of butter

- 4 (1 ounce) squares of baking chocolate

- 2 3/4 cups of semi-sweet chocolate chips

- 2 tablespoons of instant espresso powder (optional)

Directions:

1. Whisk the heavy cream with butter, bakin chocolate, chocolate chips, and espress powder in a saucepan over medium heat.

2. Let it cook until all your chocolate has melted into a smooth and thick mixture.

3. Remove it from the heat, transfer it to a bowl, and let it chill in the refrigerator until the mixture hardens for around 1 hour.

4. Prepare a baking sheet, then scoop small balls from the chocolate mixture onto the waxed paper. Store in refrigerator until the balls harden completely. Store in a cool, dry place.

Nutrition:

- Calories: 87 kcal

- Fat: 7.1 g

- Carbohydrates: 6.8 g

- Sugar: 6.8 g

- Fiber: 0

- Protein: 1.2 g

- Cholesterol: 9 mg

- Sodium: 6 mg

- Calcium: 1%

Chapter 13. Top Superfood Recipes for Thyroid Health

44. Chicken Fajita with Cauliflower Rice

Preparation Time: 15 Minutes

Cooking Time: 15 Minutes

Servings: 2

Ingredients:

- 2 large skinless, boneless chicken breasts

- 1 tbsp. of oil (like grapeseed)

- 1 small red onion, sliced thinly

- 1 avocado, peeled, pit removed, and sliced

- 3 bell peppers, red, orange, and yellow

- 1 cup of fresh tomatoes, chopped

- 1 cup of cauliflower rice

Marinade:

- 2 tbsp. of lime juice or lemon juice

- 2 tbsp. of olive oil

- 2 cloves garlic, minced

- 1/2 tsp. of sea salt

- 1/2 tsp. of ground cumin

- 1/2 tsp. of chili powder

- 1/2 tsp smoked paprika

- 1/4 cup of chopped cilantro

Directions:

1. Prep your chicken breasts by cutting them into suitable thicknesses.

2. Mix the marinade ingredients together and add them to the chicken breasts. Let it marinate for 2-6 hours and no more than 8 hours.

3. Slice and chop the vegetables (onions, peppers, and tomatoes).

4. Cook the cauliflower rice.

5. Heat oil in a suitable skillet to cook the chicke breasts, each side for about 5-7 minute (longer if breasts are thicker).

6. Meanwhile, sauté the peppers and onions.

7. Assemble the bowls with the cauliflower rice peppers, onions, and tomatoes.

8. Peel and slice avocado last to prever browning. Add chicken to the dish, drizzle wit pan juices and serve immediately.

Nutrition:

- Calories: 432 kcal

- Carbohydrates: 24g

- Protein: 28g

- Fat: 25g

- Saturated Fat: 3g

- Cholesterol: 72mg

- Sodium: 755mg

- Fiber: 7g

- Sugar: 13g

- Calcium: 5.5%

45.   Korean Sea Weed Soup

Preparation Time: 30 Minutes

Cooking Time: 15 Minutes

Servings: 4

Ingredients:

- 1 (1 ounce) package of dried brown seaweed

- 1/4-pound of beef top sirloin, minced

- 2 teaspoons of sesame oil

- 1 1/2 tablespoons of soy sauce

- 1 teaspoon of salt, or to taste

- 6 cups of water

- 1 teaspoon of minced garlic

Directions:

1. Soak the seaweed in water and cover it. Let it submerge until it becomes soft, then drain and cut into two-inch pieces.

2. In a hot saucepan (medium heat), add the beef, 1 tbsp. of soy sauce, sesame oil, and a little salt, and let it cook for 2 minutes.

3. Add in seaweed and the remaining tbsp. of so
   sauce and let it cook for 1 minute while stirrin
   frequently.

4. Add 2 cups of water and bring to a boil. Stir i
   garlic and the remaining 4 cups of water. Let
   boil, then cover and reduce heat.

5. Simmer for 20 minutes. Season to taste wit
   salt.

Nutrition:

- Calories: 65

- Fat: 3.7 g

- Carbohydrates: 1 g

- Sugar: 0.8

- Fiber: 0.1

- Protein: 6.8 g

- Cholesterol: 17 mg

- Sodium: 940 mg

- Calcium: 4%

Chapter 14.   Side Dishes and Desserts

46.   Coconut Rice Pudding

Preparation Time: 5 minutes

Cooking Time: 25 minutes

Servings: 8

Ingredients:

- 2 cups of jasmine rice

- 4-1/2 unsweetened coconut milk

- 2 Tbsps. of coconut cream

- 2 tsp. of ground cinnamon

- 2 Tbsps. of maple syrup

- 1/2 tsp. of ground turmeric

- 1-1/2 tsp. of vanilla extract

- 1/2 tsp. of ground ginger

- 1/2 cup of golden raisins

- 1/2 tsp. of coconut extract

Directions:

1. Pour 3-1/2 cups of coconut milk beverage into an instant pot and add the jasmine rice. Cover the lid tightly and cook at high pressure for 3 minutes. After which, use natural release pressure for ten minutes, then use quick pressure release to remove any pressure leftover.

2. Stir in the maple syrup, coconut cream, turmeric, ground cinnamon, golden raisins, coconut, and vanilla extract.

3. The leftover coconut milk beverage should be used at your discretion; it depends on whether you like your pudding thick or runny.

4. Serve as desired.

Nutrition:

- Calories: 30 kcal

- Carbs: 7g

- Fat: 0g

- Protein: 0g

47.   Fruit Spring Rolls

Preparation Time: 15 minutes

Cooking Time: 0 minutes

Servings: 20

Ingredients:

Spring Rolls:

- 1 cup of sliced strawberries

- 1 cup of blueberries

- 1 cup of watermelon, sliced diagonally into matchsticks

- 1 small zucchini, spiralized

- 2 lemons, zested

- 1 can no-salt-added beets, juice drained and reserved

- 1/4 cup of mint, freshly chopped

- 20 rice paper rolls

Mint Dip:

- 1/2 cup of strawberries, sliced

- 1 Tbsps. of mint leaves

- 1/2 cup of coconut milk-yogurt

- 1/2 tsp. of lemon juice

Directions:

1. In a small bowl, mix 1/2 cup of water and 1/2 cup beet juice.

2. Moisten your work surface (cutting board) to prevent the rice paper from sticking to the surface.

3. Dip the rice paper roll into the water and beet juice mixture for 20 seconds. It will become pliable but still be firm.

4. Lay the paper roll on the wet cutting board, then add the ingredients quickly. Start with the strawberries, then watermelon, watermelon, mint, finish with the zucchini.

5. Roll quickly to ensure your wrapper doesn't lose moisture or become mushy, and ensure the wrapper isn't overfilled. To roll the wrapper, start by stretching the left side of the wrapper over the ingredients, tuck it in, roll for a bit, then tuck in the top and bottom flaps, and then keep rolling until you reach the edge of the other side.

6. Repeat steps 3-5 for as many rolls as possible.

7. For the mint dip, blend the yogurt, mint, strawberries, and lemon juice in a food processor for 90 seconds. Pair with spring roll and enjoy.

- Calories: 131 kcal

- Carbs: 18g

- Fat: 3g

- Protein: 9g

48. Deep-fried Zucchini

Preparation Time: 5 minutes

Cooking Time: 15 minutes

Servings: 6

Ingredients:

- 4 medium zucchinis, trimmed and sliced

- 3 cups of Sunflower oil

- 1/4 cup of cornstarch

- 3/4 cup of all-purpose flour

- 1/4 tsp. of pepper

- 1 tsp. of salt, divided

Directions:

1. Add the sunflower oil to a deep skillet until it is about 3 inches deep, then place over medium heat.

2. Mix the flour, 1/2 teaspoon of salt, cornstarch and pepper in a bowl, then dredge the Zucchini in the flour and shake off the excess.

3. When the oil reaches about 370 °F, add the flour-coated zucchini to the oil and fry for 2 minutes, then arrange on a tray with paper towels to absorb excess oil.

4. Season with salt to taste and serve immediately.

Nutrition:

- Calories: 320kcal

- Carbs: 12g

- Fat: 29g

- Protein: 8g

49.   Frozen Banana Bites

Preparation Time: 20 minutes

Cooking Time: 2 hours 15 minutes

Servings: 48 bites

Ingredients:

- A cup of peanut butter

- 1/3 cup of toffee baking bits

- 1 oz. of semisweet chocolate

- 4 bananas (cut into rounds of one-inch thickness)

- 1 tbsp. of shortening

Directions:

1. First, take wax paper and cover the baking sheet.

2. Then, take each slice of banana and layer with one spoon of peanut butter. Take a toothpick and insert it through the banana piercing through the layer of peanut butter. Then, take the banana bites and arrange them nicely on the baking sheet. Freeze the preparation for at least thirty minutes or overnight.

3. Now, melt the chocolate and keep stirring it frequently. To avoid any form of scorching, use a spatula to scrape down the sides continuously.

4. Take another waxed paper to cover another baking sheet.

5. Take two to four bites of bananas from the freezer and then use the chocolate mixture to coat them. Now, take the coated bites and place them on the baking sheet that you just covered with wax paper. On top of each coated banana, sprinkle some toffee bits. Do the same process with all the bites. Now, return the preparation into the freezer and keep it there for at least an hour. Before serving, keep the bites at room temperature for around ten to fifteen minutes.

Nutrition:

- Calories: 76 kcal

- Protein: 1.8g

- Fat: 5.1g

- Carbs: 6.9g

- Fiber: 1g

50.   Italian Kale Chips

Preparation Time: 5 minutes

Cooking Time: 15 minutes

Servings: 2 servings

Ingredients:

- 4 cups of kale (stems removed, loosely torn)

- 1-eighth tsp. each of

- Salt

- Pepper

- Garlic powder

- 1/4 tsp. of Italian seasoning

- 1 tbsp. of olive oil

- 1 tbsp. of grated Parmesan cheese (Optional)

Directions:

1. Set the temperature of the oven to 225 °F and preheat. The oven temperature is very important in this recipe; otherwise, your kale chips might just get burnt.

2. Now, it is time to prepare the kale. Tear the leaves and remove the stems. The leaves should be torn into bite-sized pieces.

3. Then, take a baking sheet and use cooking spray to coat it. After that, take the kale leaves and arrange them on the sheet in a single layer. Drizzle some more oil. Remember that too much oil can make the kale chips soggy, so be aware of how much oil you are using.

4. Now, take a small-sized bowl, in it, add garlic powder, Italian seasoning, pepper, and salt, and mix them together. After mixing thoroughly, sprinkle this mixture evenly over the kale.

5. Once all of this is done, take the kale preparation and bake it for twelve minutes. After that, take them out, toss them a bit so that they get turned, and then return the preparation to the oven again. Bake for another five to ten minutes. By this time, the kale should be crispy. But keep a close eye on them since you don't want them burnt.

6. Once done, remove, and if you want, then sprinkle some grated Parmesan on top.

Nutrition:

- Calories: 148kcal

- Protein: 6g

- Fat: 9g

- Carbs: 15g

- Fiber: 5g

eemed liable for any hardship or damages that may befall them after ndertaking information described herein.

Additionally, the information in the following pages is intended only for nformational purposes and should thus be thought of as universal. As efitting its nature, it is presented without assurance regarding its rolonged validity or interim quality. Trademarks that are mentioned are one without written consent and can in no way be considered an ndorsement from the trademark holder.

CPSIA information can be obtained
at www.ICGtesting.com
Printed in the USA
BVHW041202240321
603332BV00008B/1227